LIGHTNING
BOLT
BOOKS™

Whale Sharks
in Action

Benjamin Tunby

Lerner Publications • Minneapolis

To Aili and Nolan

Lerner Publications Company
A division of Lerner Publishing Group, Inc.
241 First Avenue North
Minneapolis, MN 55401 USA

For reading levels and more information, look up this title at www.lernerbooks.com.

Library of Congress Cataloging-in-Publication Data

Names: Tunby, Benjamin.
Title: Whale sharks in action / Benjamin Tunby.
Description: Minneapolis : Lerner Publications, [2018] | Series: Lightning bolt books. Shark world | Audience: Age 6-9. | Audience: K to grade 3. | Includes bibliographical references and index.
Identifiers: LCCN 2016045729 (print) | LCCN 2016046919 (ebook) | ISBN 9781512433821 (lb : alk. paper) | ISBN 9781512455984 (pb : alk. paper) | ISBN 9781512450651 (eb pdf)
Subjects: LCSH: Whale shark—Juvenile literature. | Sharks—Juvenile literature.
Classification: LCC QL638.95.R4 T86 2018 (print) | LCC QL638.95.R4 (ebook) | DDC 597.3/3—dc23

LC record available at https://lccn.loc.gov/2016045729

Manufactured in the United States of America
1-42018-23888-12/12/2016

Table of Contents

The Biggest Fish

A whale shark swims in the ocean. It glides with its mouth open. The giant fish pulls water and tiny animals into its mouth.

Whale sharks have powerful tails and lots of fins. Their tails push them through the water. Their fins help them turn and balance.

Whale sharks may grow as long as 60 feet (18 meters).

Whale sharks are the largest known fish. An adult is about 40 feet (12 m) long. That is the length of a school bus!

Whale sharks live in oceans around the world. They stay in warm waters. The huge fish swim near coasts and in the open ocean.

Whale Shark Life Cycle

A whale shark mother doesn't lay eggs in water as many fish do. Whale shark babies grow in eggs inside their mother. They hatch inside her too.

Whale sharks give birth to live babies. Whale shark babies are called pups.

A whale shark pup looks like a small adult. It is ready to find its own food right away.

A whale shark pup is about 18 inches (46 centimeters) long when it is born. That is the size of a human baby at birth.

A whale shark is ready to have pups when it is twenty to thirty years old. It may have as many as three hundred pups at a time!

Whale sharks can live for one hundred years.

Big Mouth and Spots

Whale sharks have spots on their backs. Every shark's spots make a unique pattern.

People don't know what whale sharks do with their teeth. These fish don't bite or chew their food.

A whale shark has 300 to 350 rows of small teeth. One shark can have more than 3,000 tiny teeth.

Whale sharks have big mouths. Their mouths can be almost 5 feet (1.5 m) wide. They need big mouths to eat and breathe.

Whoosh! A whale shark pulls water into its mouth. Gills take oxygen from the water. The water goes out through gill slits on the sides of the head.

Do you see the gill slits on this whale shark's head?

Into the Deep

Whale sharks are predators. They eat plankton, fish eggs, small fish, and squid.

Plankton are tiny plants and animals in the ocean. Most plankton are so small that you can't see them.

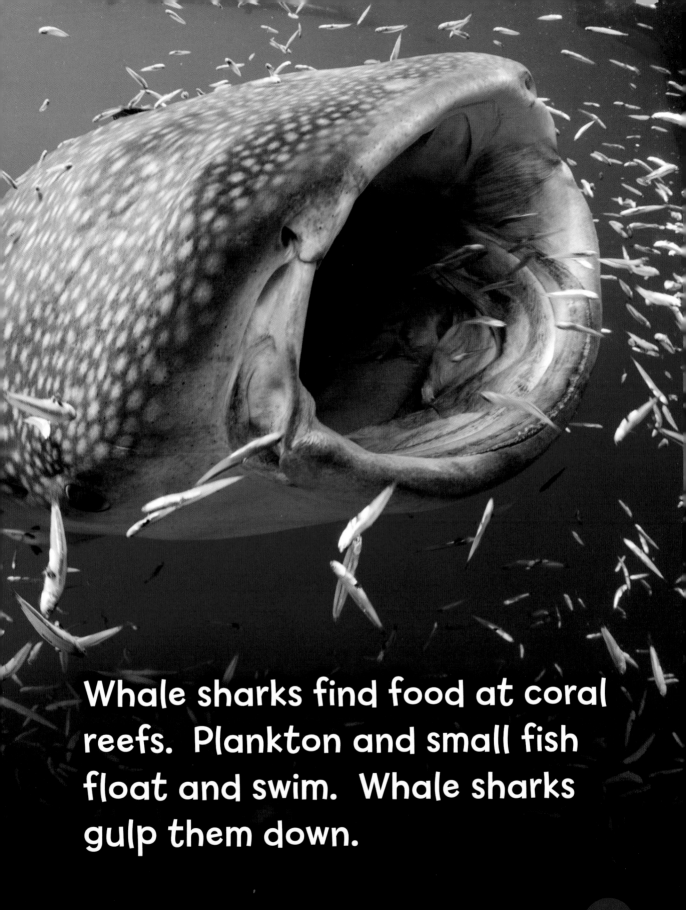

Whale sharks find food at coral reefs. Plankton and small fish float and swim. Whale sharks gulp them down.

Whale sharks take water and plankton into their mouths. The water passes over pads in their heads. The pads catch the plankton.

Whale sharks usually stay near the surface of the water. They can dive about 6,000 feet (1,829 m) deep in search of food. Whale sharks are giant filters of the sea!

Diagram

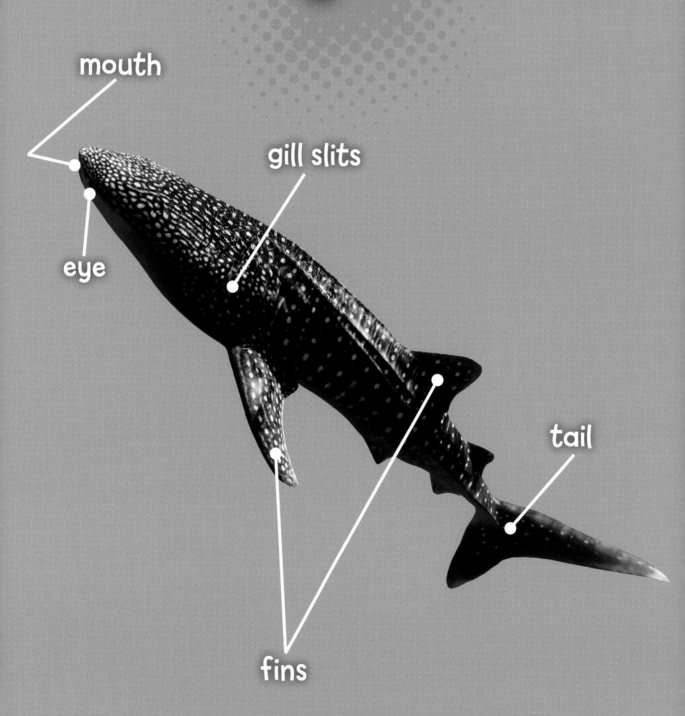

mouth

gill slits

eye

tail

fins

Whale Sharks and People

- The whale shark is important in the Philippines. It is a national symbol. It even appears on the country's money.

- Fishing is the biggest threat to whale sharks. People eat whale shark meat. Many countries have laws banning whale shark fishing.

- Whale sharks don't attack humans. People dive to get close to the big fish. Some whale sharks will allow divers to touch them.

Glossary

coast: the land near a sea or an ocean

coral reef: a hard ridge in the ocean where many animals and plants live

filter: something that removes small items from water

gill: an organ used by fish to get oxygen from water

gill slit: an opening on the side of a whale shark's head through which water passes

oxygen: a gas that animals need to breathe

plankton: small living things that float in water

predator: an animal that eats another animal

Further Reading

Berne, Emma Carlson. Whale Sharks: Bulletproof! New York: PowerKids, 2014.

Discovery Kids: Sharks
http://discoverykids.com/category/sharks

Enchanted Learning: Whale Shark
http://www.enchantedlearning.com/subjects/sharks/species/Whaleshark.shtml

Fleisher, Paul. *Ocean Food Webs in Action*. Minneapolis: Lerner Publications, 2014.

Nelson, Kristin L. *Let's Look at Sharks*. Minneapolis: Lerner Publications, 2011.

Shingu, Susumu. *Wandering Whale Sharks*. Berkeley, CA: Owlkids Books, 2015.

Index

Photo Acknowledgments

The images in this book are used with the permission of: © torstenvelden/Getty Images, p. 2, 12; © James D. Morgan/Getty Images, p. 4; © Pete Oxford/Minden Pictures, pp. 5, 6; © Peter Verhoog/Minden Pictures, pp. 7, 15; © Michele Westmorland/Getty Images, p. 8; © Alex Mustard/NPL/Minden Pictures, pp. 9, 11; © Brian J. Skerry/Getty Images, p. 10; © Jurgen Freund/NPL/Minden Pictures, p. 13; © Reinhard Dirscherl/Alamy, pp. 14, 17, 18; © D.P. Wilson/Minden Pictures, p. 16; © Tim Fitzharris/Minden Pictures, p. 19; © Jason Edwards/Getty Images, p. 20; © Andrey Nekrasov/Alamy, p. 23.

Cover: © iStockphoto.com/Krzysztof Odziomek.

Main body text set in Billy Infant regular 28/36. Typeface provided by SparkType.